FOR

FROM

1

MY
FAVORITE
COLOR IS
F*CK
YOU

2

F*CK YOU
VERY MUCH

3

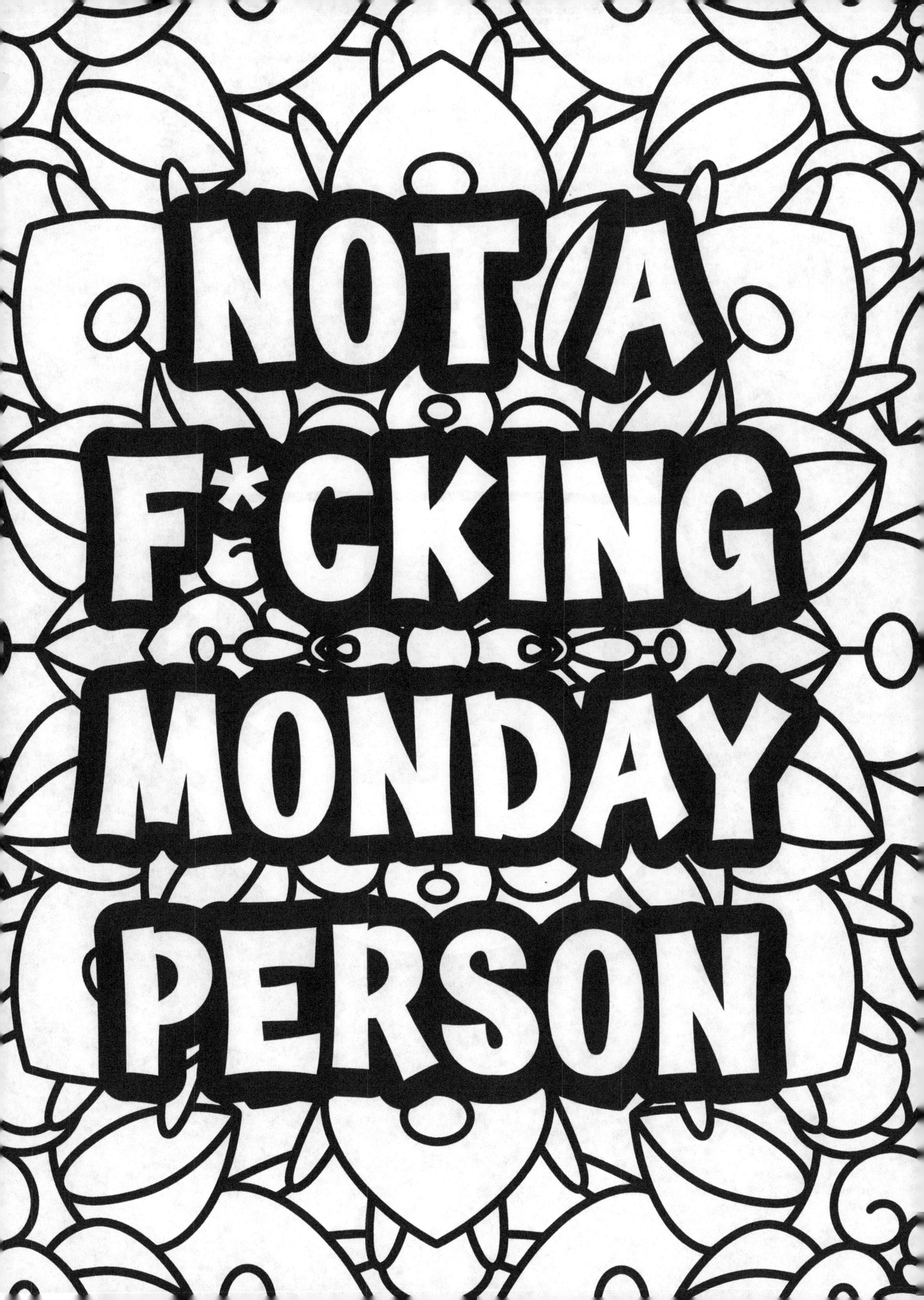
NOT A
F*CKING
MONDAY
PERSON

4

INHALE
GOOD
SH*T
EXHALE
BULLSH*T

5

TOO MUCH
SH*T
GOING
ON RIGHT
NOW

6

NOT
GIVING A
F*CK IS
BETTER
THAN
REVENGE

7

CHEER
THE
FUCK
UP

8

FUCK
MY BIG
SANTA
BALLS

9

LET
THAT
SH*T
GO

10

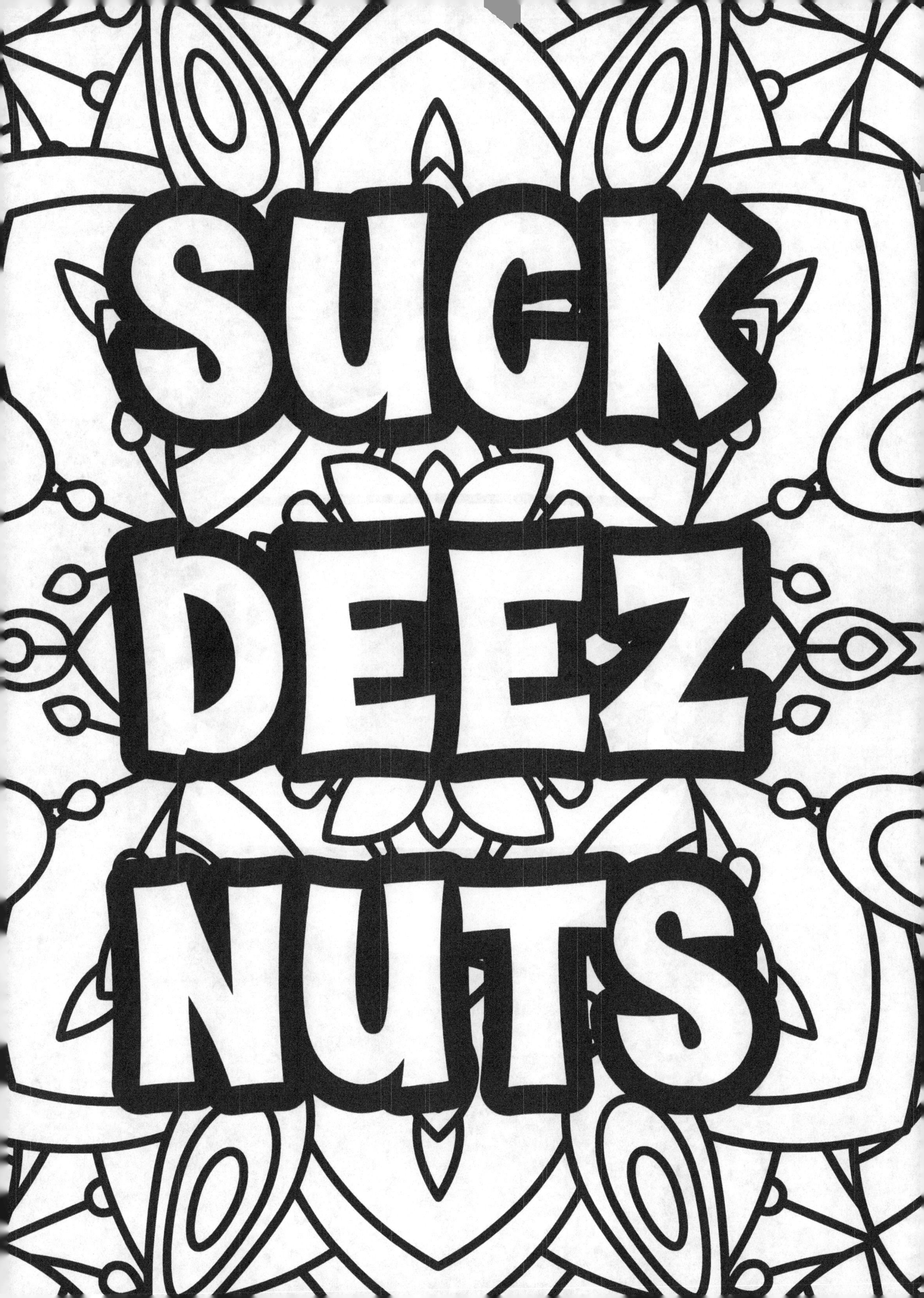
SUCK
DEEZ
NUTS

11

SCREW THIS

12

FRIDAY
IS MY
SECOND
FAVORITE
F WORD

13

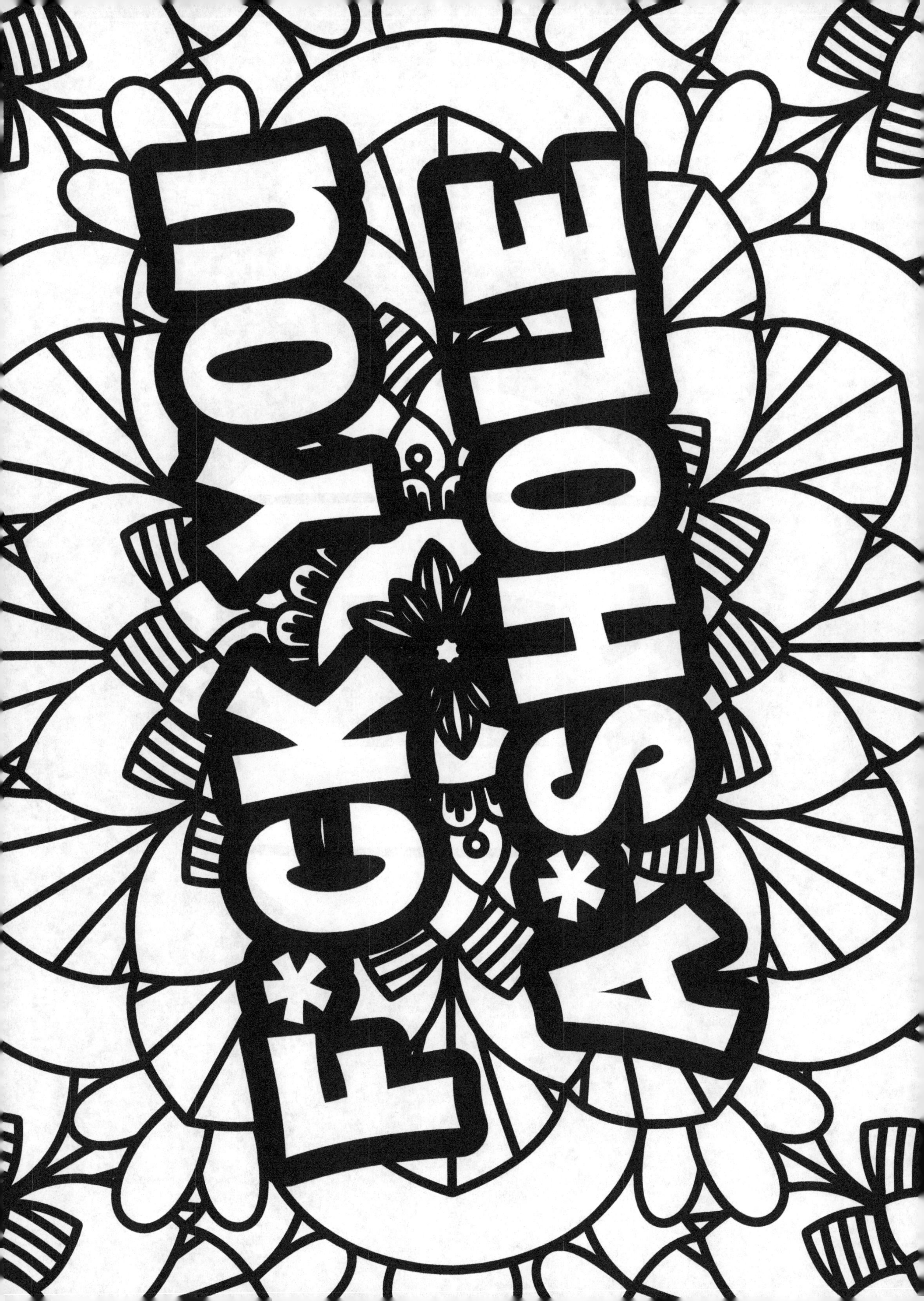
F*CK YOU
A*SHOLE

14

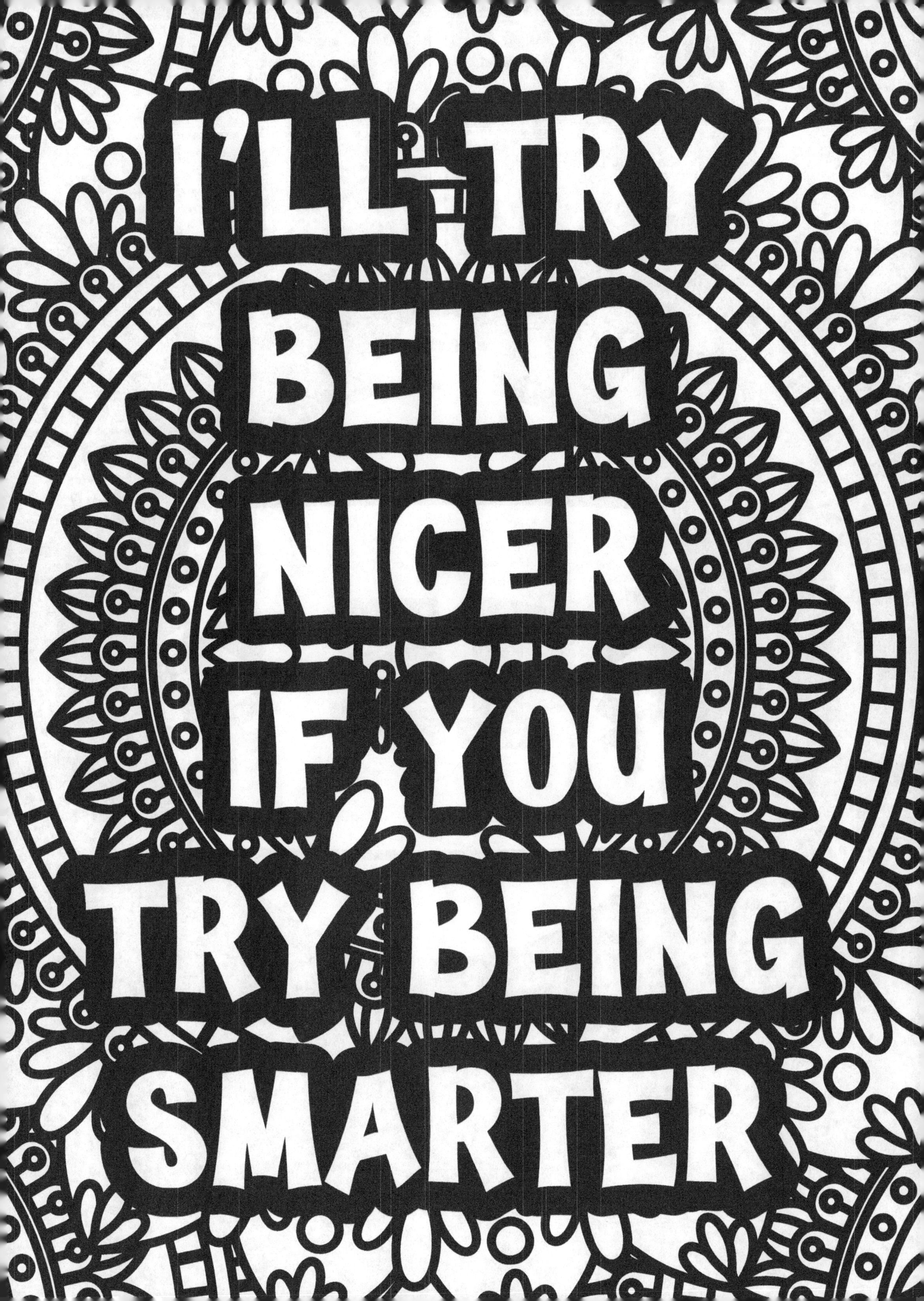
I'LL TRY BEING NICER IF YOU TRY BEING SMARTER

15

HOW
ABOUT
NEVER
???

16

WHAT
THE
ACTUAL
F*CK???

17

I DON'T
GIVE A
DAMN
SH*T

18

SORRY
I DON'T
GIVE A
F*CK

19

MERRY
F*CKING
CHRISTMAS

20

DON'T
LIKE THE
WAY YOU
TALK
TO ME

21

F*CK
YOU
PUS*Y

22

YOU
F*CKING
STINK
SH*T

23

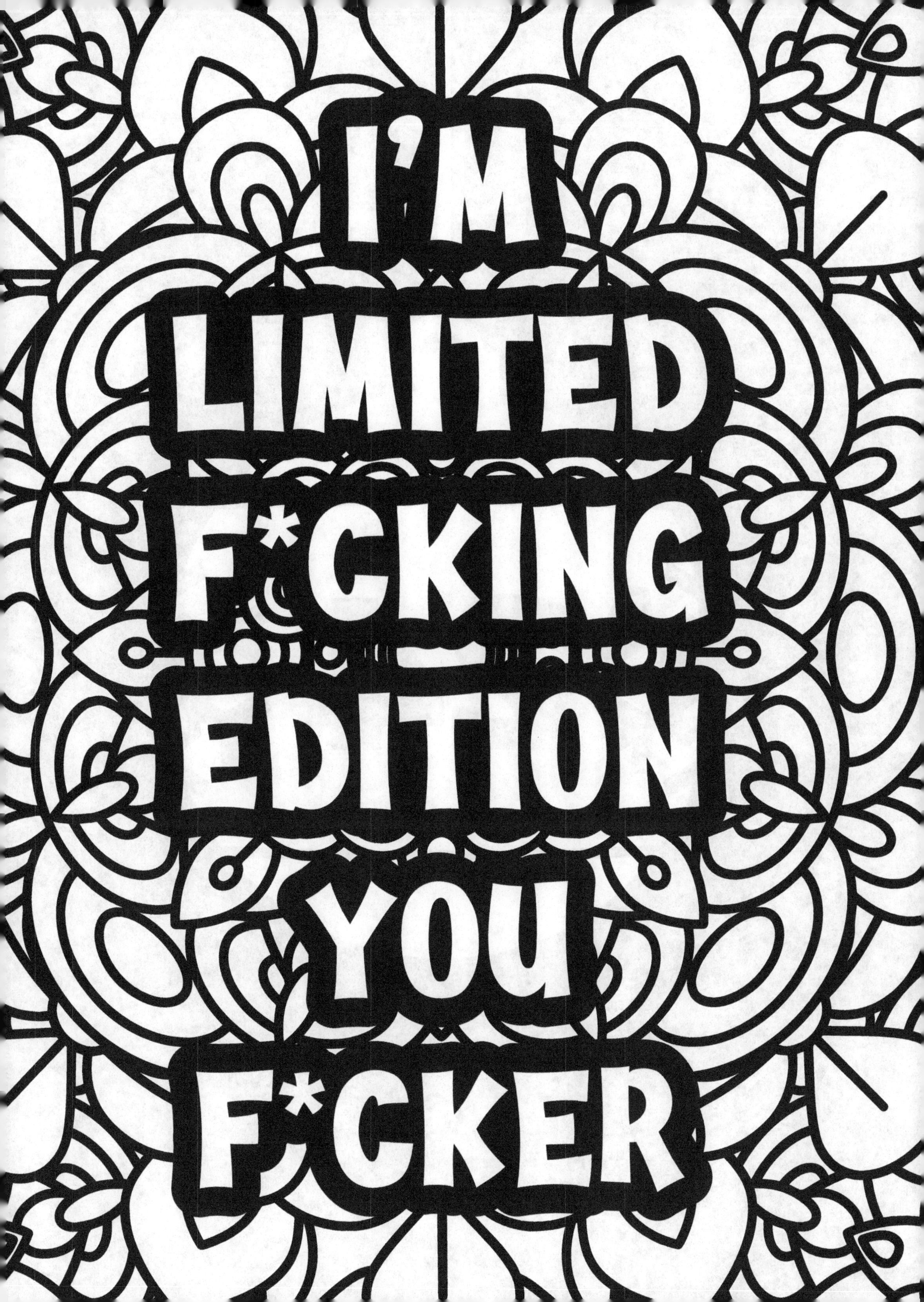
I'M
LIMITED
F*CKING
EDITION
YOU
F*CKER

24

LET'S
F*CK
THIS
SHIT UP

25

BITCH
BEE
GONE
!!!

Made in the USA
Las Vegas, NV
27 November 2023

81682379R00031